Why does plastic hurt the planet?

Written by Clive Gifford

Illustrated by Hannah Li

Foreword by Dr. Tridibesh Dey, Aarhus University

EARTHAWARE
KIDS

A message from Dr. Tridibesh Dey, Aarhus University

Tridibesh is a plastic scientist, and has also trained as an engineer. He studies plastic in everyday life, and has helped recycle plastic in the villages and cities of India. He works with other scientists, experts, and world leaders to tackle the problems of plastic pollution.

Plastic is a word used for a wide range of materials made of chemicals. It is a serious problem because more plastic is being made than can safely be dealt with, leading to widespread pollution. This is affecting everything on the planet, including all living things.

Plastic is long-lasting, and its remains are being discovered everywhere—in air, water, and soil. They are increasingly combining with living things and have even been discovered in the human body and blood. Scientists have found that many of the chemicals common in plastic can cause serious illness.

There is a lot that we can all do to stop more harm from happening. Avoiding and reducing the use of plastic in everyday life, like in packaging, can make a big difference. It can encourage producers and companies to look for plastic replacements. Recycling can help, too. We can all ask people in government to have stronger controls on plastic production and chemical use. Speak to your friends, learn from each other, and spread the word in your local area and beyond. Last but not the least, you can have an active interest in science, technology, and communities to help to solve some of the problems of plastic.

When you have read this book and learned about the different parts of the complicated plastic problem, please share your knowledge and thoughts with others. Let your voice be heard and believe that, together, we can bring change. Our future depends on it.

Contents

Mind mapping 4

What is the problem with plastic?   6

Lasting forever 8
Single-use 10
Land pollution 12
Landfill 14
Wasting resources 16

Where does plastic come from?   18

Plastic up close 20
How plastics are made 22

Why do we use plastic?   24

Inside and outdoors 26
Light, tough, and cheap 28
Easily shaped 30

Why is plastic in the ocean?   32

Traveling out to sea 34
Creating microplastics 36
Shoreline to seafloor 38

Is plastic harming the ocean?   40

Connecting currents 42
Sea life 44
Microplastic food chains 46

How do we start to clear up?   48

Cleaning up 50
Science and technology 52
Banning plastics 54

Can we stop using plastic?   56

A less plastic life 58
Recycling 60
Alternative materials 62

What else can we do?   64

What can we all do? 66
What can you do? 68

Glossary 70
Index 72

Mind mapping

The reason this book is called Mind Mappers is because it is organized like a mind map. A mind map is a picture diagram that connects lots of different ideas. It is a very useful way to make complicated topics easy to understand. The mind map on this page looks at the question that is the title of this book—why does plastic hurt the planet? It divides the subject into the eight further questions, which are at the beginning of each chapter.

Follow the lines

Find the question that you would like to explore and follow the colored lines to look at the individual topics. For example, there are two main ways to stop using plastic—by avoiding using plastic altogether and choosing to buy alternative materials instead. Keep following the lines to see how these topics subdivide.

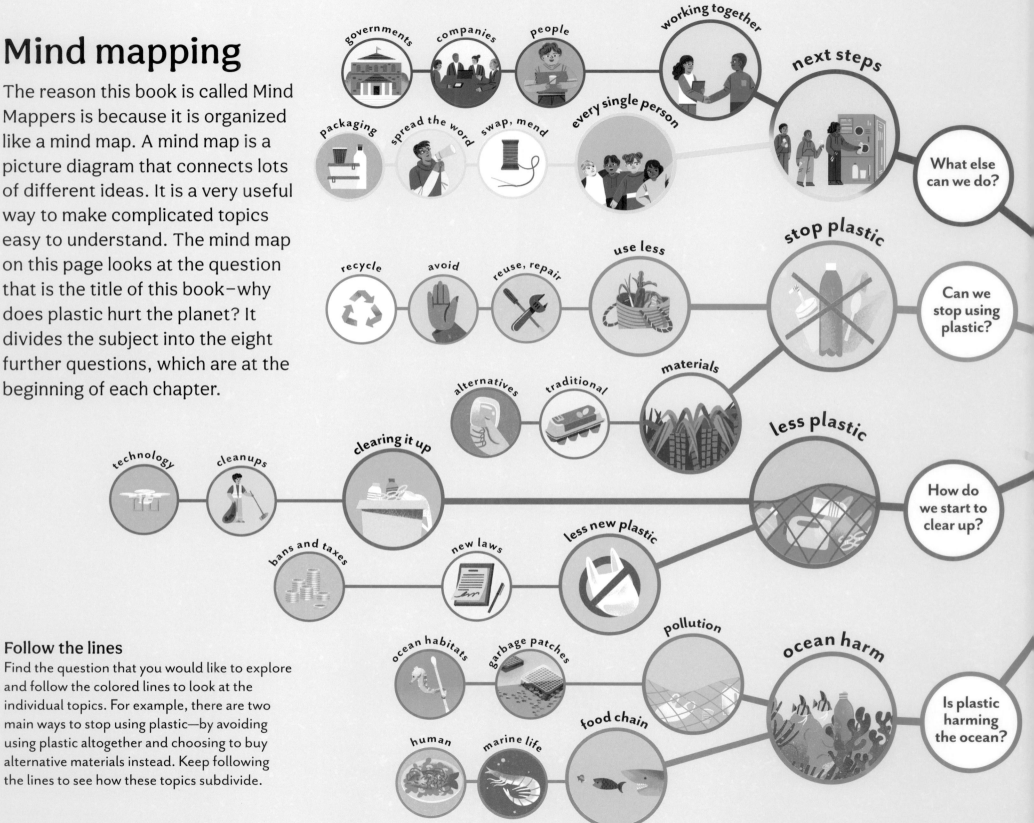

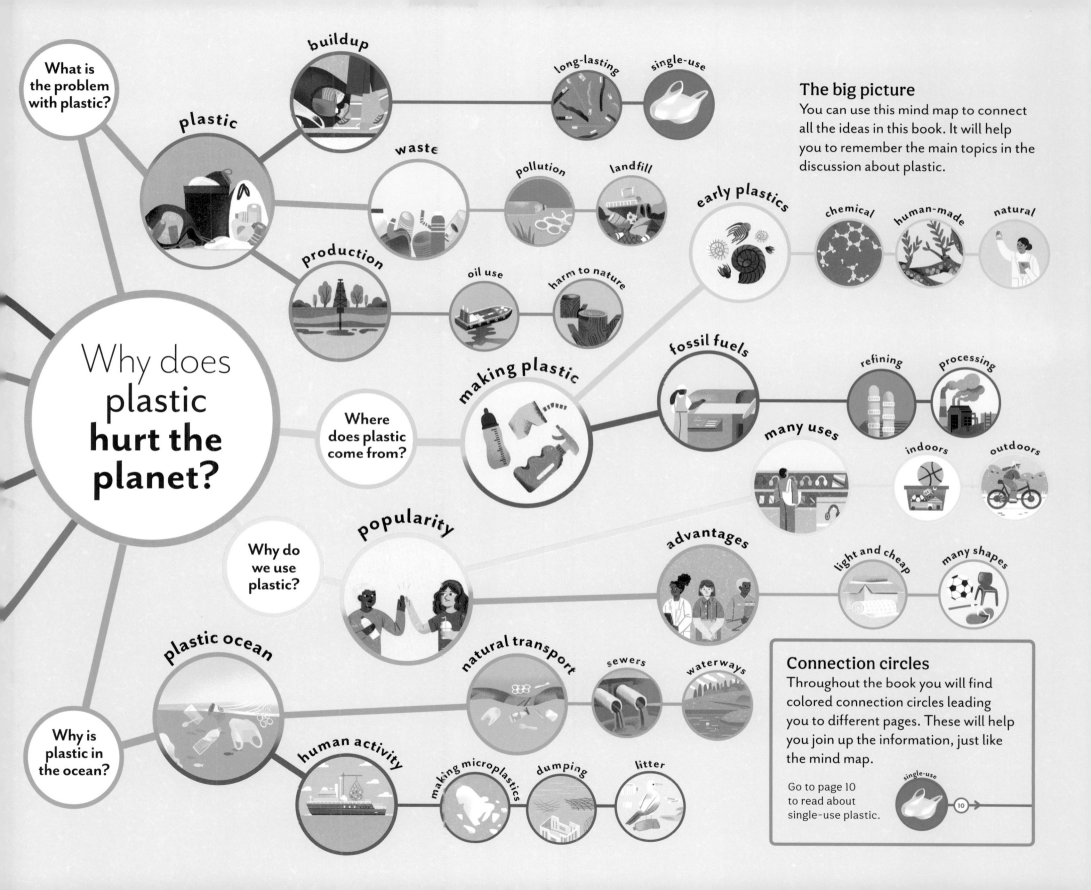

What is the problem with plastic?

plastic

buildup

long-lasting

single-use

waste

pollution

landfill

early plastics

chemical

human-made

natural

production

oil use

harm to nature

The big picture
You can use this mind map to connect all the ideas in this book. It will help you to remember the main topics in the discussion about plastic.

Why does plastic **hurt the planet?**

Where does plastic come from?

making plastic

fossil fuels

refining

processing

many uses

indoors

outdoors

Why do we use plastic?

popularity

advantages

light and cheap

many shapes

plastic ocean

natural transport

sewers

waterways

Why is plastic in the ocean?

human activity

making microplastics

dumping

litter

Connection circles
Throughout the book you will find colored connection circles leading you to different pages. These will help you join up the information, just like the mind map.

Go to page 10 to read about single-use plastic.

single-use

10

what is the
problem with
plastic?

We make and use hundreds of millions of tons of plastic every year. It is extremely useful, but hangs around long after it is thrown away. It clutters up our land, rivers, and oceans, and causes harm to many living things and ecosystems.

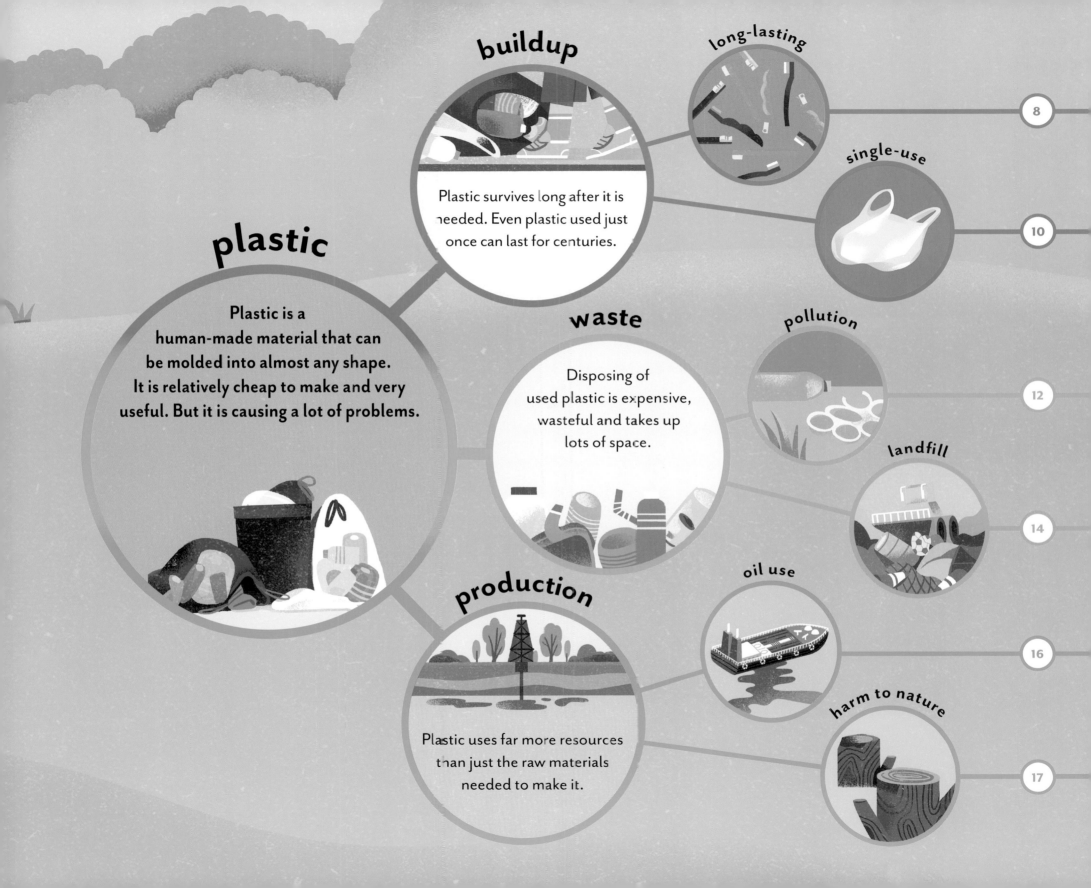

plastic

Plastic is a human-made material that can be molded into almost any shape. It is relatively cheap to make and very useful. But it is causing a lot of problems.

buildup

Plastic survives long after it is needed. Even plastic used just once can last for centuries.

long-lasting 8

single-use 10

waste

Disposing of used plastic is expensive, wasteful and takes up lots of space.

pollution 12

landfill 14

production

Plastic uses far more resources than just the raw materials needed to make it.

oil use 16

harm to nature 17

Lasting forever

Plastics last a long time, and this has made them very popular. People marvel at how durable and robust plastics are compared to many other materials. But this big benefit comes at a cost. Plastics, and the harmful chemicals they can contain, stay around long after they have stopped being useful and have been thrown away.

Nutrients released from rotting materials enrich the soil with useful substances.

Biodegrading

Fruit, vegetables, and natural materials such as paper and cotton rot away. They biodegrade, or decay, into simpler substances that are absorbed into the soil.

An apple takes 4–8 weeks to biodegrade.

Decomposers

Worms, millipedes, bacteria, and fungi such as mushrooms help break down rotting materials into simpler substances. Some of these chemicals, including nitrogen and phosphorus, are recycled, helping plants grow well in soil.

Nature's cleanup

It can take just weeks for many natural materials to break down into the environment. Human-made objects usually take much longer.

14

landfill

Paper made from trees takes around 6 weeks to break down.

Most fruit and vegetables take just a few weeks to rot away.

Cotton clothes take up to five months to decompose.

Still here

Much of the plastic produced in the last 120 years has not yet broken down fully in nature. As a result, waste is mounting up.

500+ years
Plastic toothbrushes

20–50 years
A single-use plastic bag

Breaking down

Plastics do not decompose, or break down, easily. They take their time. Plastics may first break down into tiny pieces known as microplastics, but it can take hundreds of years for them to decompose fully.

450 years
PET plastic bottles

Around 400 years
Plastic ring carriers

Plastic connections

Nature's way of recycling does not work well for plastic. Decomposers cannot break down plastic like they can with natural materials such as food and paper.

Up to 200 years
Plastic drinking straws

50 years or more
Styrofoam plastic cups

Single-use

More than a third of all the plastic produced each year is used to make items such as bags, bottles, wrappers, and straws. Many of these things are used just once or for a few moments, then thrown away. Cotton swabs are used for less time than it took to make them! This wasteful way of consuming resources also creates mountains of plastic rubbish and pollution.

Stretchy single-use plastic balloons hang around long after they have burst or deflated.

Use and bin

Some people treat reusable items as single-use. Festivalgoers sometimes abandon their plastic tents and costumes, creating lots of extra waste.

Paper or not?

Some single-use plastics hide inside containers made of other materials. Card cartons for juice, milk, and some foods have a lining made of plastic. The cartons are used only once before going in the trash.

Plastic bags

Most flimsy plastic bags get less than 15 minutes' use before being thrown away. As litter, they can be blown long distances across land or into rivers.

microplastics

36

Glitter

Most glitter is made of PET plastic and aluminum metal. It may be tiny, but this microplastic is hard to get rid of. When it is washed off, glitter can flow through waterways and travel out to sea.

Coffee convenience

Billions of single-use polystyrene cups are used and thrown away each year. They cannot be recycled.

Fast-food packaging

Plastic forks, straws, burger boxes, and french fry trays are only used for as long as it takes to gobble down a quick meal, then discarded.

Plastic connections

Single-use plastic is everywhere! It is used in vast numbers every single day. If we can avoid making and using it, we can help to stop plastic from filling up garbage dumps and polluting the land and the sea.

Land pollution

Unwanted plastic causes many problems when it is thrown away as litter. While litter can ruin the look of a landscape, it can do even more harm to the plants and creatures that live there. Plastic bags or sheets might cover plants and stop them getting the sunlight they need to flourish. Insects, frogs, and baby birds can get trapped inside plastic containers. Toxic chemicals in plastic can also pollute soil and water.

Attractive meals

Many creatures are attracted to brightly colored plastic, thinking it is food. When eaten, the plastic can stick in their throat or gut and make them ill or even die.

Lethal lids

Birds with long bills may spear a plastic coffee cup lid, which they then struggle to remove. The lid stops them from closing their bill, meaning the bird cannot eat or drink properly unless rescued.

Entangled

Plastics such as netting, cord, and fishing line can take centuries to rot away. They cause misery and injury to the birds and small mammals that get tangled up in them.

Fire threat

Some plastics can be set on fire by a spark, lightning, or a burning match or cigarette. These plastics burn quickly and give off poisonous fumes. They can also set dry grasses and wood alight, causing a wildfire.

Ring carriers

Plastic ring carriers hold cans together. They can get stuck around the necks of birds and mammals, and strangle them unless they are helped.

Plastic connections

Plastic's durability and toughness can cause real problems for wildlife. Keeping our countryside free of plastic litter improves the chances that a wide range of species can flourish.

Countryside cleanup

Plastic is often left behind after a countryside walk or picnic. Unless we pick up our own litter and that left by others, plastic can pollute the land further.

Plastic down under

Lightweight plastics such as bags can be blown down burrows, clogging them and other animal homes.

blown away

34

Chemical harm

Some harmful chemicals seep out of plastics and enter soil and water. Scientists are studying how much harm these chemicals could cause living things.

Soil pollution

Creatures such as worms and springtails help improve soil quality by adding air and boosting nutrients. But these creatures are being threatened by growing levels of microplastics in the soil, which scientists believe could affect their growth and movement.

Landfill

The world produces more than 2 billion tons of solid waste each year—that's the weight of more than 300 million African elephants. Nearly a fifth is plastic. Where does it all go? Some is recycled or burned, but most is buried in the ground in landfill sites. These places occupy thousands of hectares of land that could be used for other purposes or left wild for nature. Plastic waste in landfill can cause many problems.

Greenhouse gas

As garbage rots away it produces methane gas, which travels into the atmosphere. Methane is one of the main greenhouse gases responsible for climate change.

Changing the environment

Landfill destroys habitats for many living things, driving some wildlife away while providing a home for disease-spreading pests, such as flies and rats.

Waste plastic

Plastic dominates landfill even though it only makes up 10—15 percent of its total weight. This is because plastic objects are lightweight but take up lots of space. Plastic waste also does not rot away quickly like paper, card, and food.

chemical harm

Burning plastic

Some plastic waste is burned at very high temperatures to reduce its size. The ash that is left behind is then buried. Burning, or incineration, can release greenhouse gases unless they are carefully filtered out, as well as small amounts of other toxic substances.

Problems for locals

Landfill sites can be expensive to look after and the smell can upset people who live nearby. They can also be noisy and are often an eyesore.

Fire hazard

Landfills are dangerous places full of sharp objects, chemicals, and fire risks. Gases found in landfills, such as methane, can catch fire easily.

Taking up space

Landfill takes up large amounts of space that could be used for other things—from parks and farmland to land for new homes. In big cities, space for landfill is running out, yet waste levels are rising.

Pollution risk

As rainwater travels through a landfill, it can collect harmful chemicals that have seeped out of plastic waste. This liquid, or leachate, can run into the soil, streams, and rivers, polluting them and harming living things far away.

greenhouse gases

Plastic connections

A huge amount of our plastic waste ends up in landfill. Its treatment there releases harmful gases and chemicals. By reducing our plastic use, we can make sure that less plastic goes there in the first place.

Wasting resources

Plastics may seem cheap to make, but they come at a high cost to the planet's natural resources and environment. Plastics are mostly made from oil, which is a nonrenewable resource. This means that when all the oil is used up, it cannot be replaced for millions of years. The large amounts of energy used in extracting oil to make and transport plastic is increasing the greenhouse effect. This is resulting in climate change.

Oil resources

Plastics use up around six percent of all the oil produced each year. The oil has to be searched for, removed, and transported. These tasks also use lots of energy and other resources.

Energy for plastic

Lots of energy is needed to refine oil, turn it into plastic, and transport the raw plastic to factories. This energy is often created by burning more oil.

Oil spills

Leaks and spills from oil wells and tanker ships can devastate seas and land. Just one oil spill can kill hundreds of sea turtles and thousands of birds.

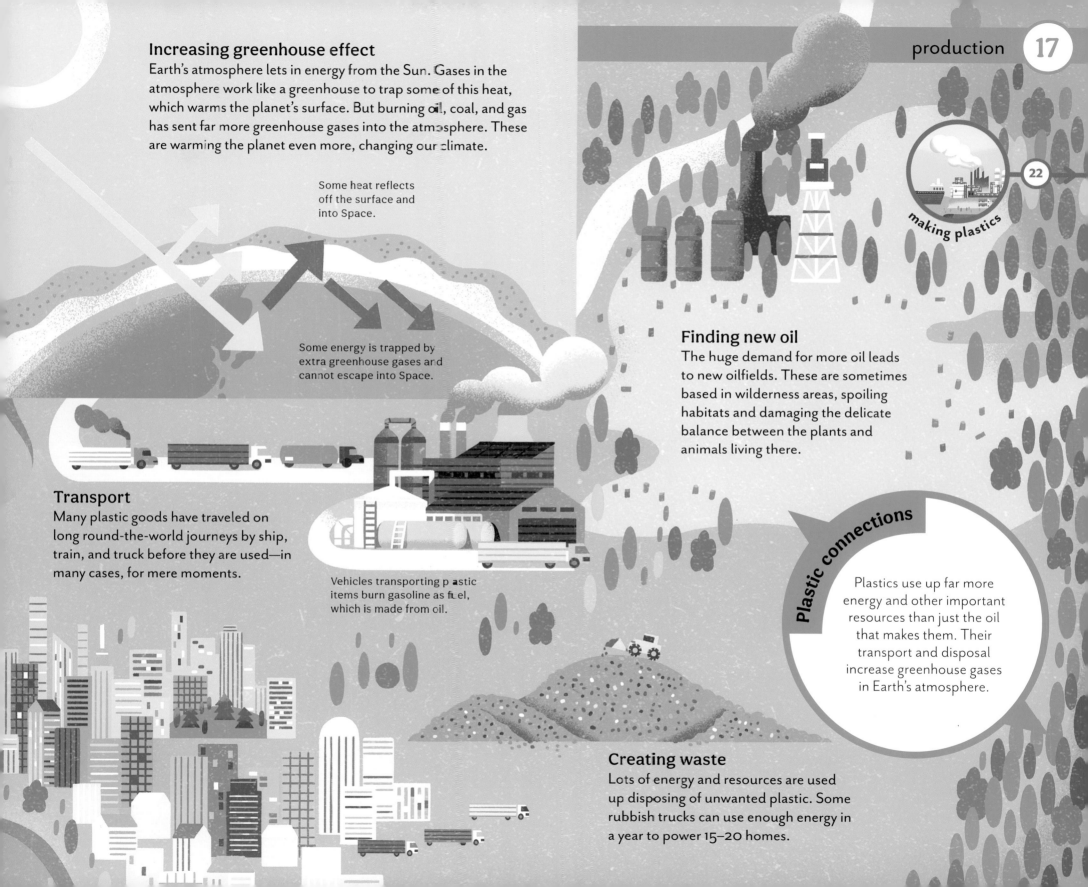

Increasing greenhouse effect

Earth's atmosphere lets in energy from the Sun. Gases in the atmosphere work like a greenhouse to trap some of this heat, which warms the planet's surface. But burning oil, coal, and gas has sent far more greenhouse gases into the atmosphere. These are warming the planet even more, changing our climate.

Some heat reflects off the surface and into Space.

Some energy is trapped by extra greenhouse gases and cannot escape into Space.

Transport

Many plastic goods have traveled on long round-the-world journeys by ship, train, and truck before they are used—in many cases, for mere moments.

Vehicles transporting plastic items burn gasoline as fuel, which is made from oil.

making plastics **22**

Finding new oil

The huge demand for more oil leads to new oilfields. These are sometimes based in wilderness areas, spoiling habitats and damaging the delicate balance between the plants and animals living there.

Plastic connections

Plastics use up far more energy and other important resources than just the oil that makes them. Their transport and disposal increase greenhouse gases in Earth's atmosphere.

Creating waste

Lots of energy and resources are used up disposing of unwanted plastic. Some rubbish trucks can use enough energy in a year to power 15–20 homes.

where
does plastic
come from?

There are many different types of plastic—from chunky, solid blocks to stretchy bands and clear, thin films. Plastic materials are extremely versatile. The more new plastics that have been invented, the more things they have been used for.

making plastic

There are thousands of different plastics. Almost all of them were invented in the 1900s. Plastic has become a big part of modern life.

early plastics

A few plastics, such as latex rubber, are found in nature. But most are synthetic materials—made by humans using chemical processes.

chemical

20

natural

20

human-made

21

fossil fuels

Almost all synthetic plastics are made from crude oil, which is extracted from underground oil reserves.

refining

22

processing

23

Plastic up close

Different types of plastic might look and feel different, and have different properties. But they all have one thing in common. They are polymers, which means they are made of long chains of repeating molecules. Each molecule is known as a monomer. In a plastic, a monomer is joined firmly to its neighbors by strong chemical bonds. A plastic can contain chains of thousands or even millions of these molecules.

Natural plastics

Types of natural plastic have been used for more than 2,500 years. People in Central America tapped latex sap from the trunks of rubber trees, which hardened into natural rubber after heating.

Patterns of atoms

Most plastics contain many carbon atoms, as well as other atoms, such as sulfur, oxygen, and hydrogen. The combination makes each plastic different—from hard-wearing PET used for tennis balls to soft LDPE plastic in sports drinks bottles.

alternative materials

62

Tortoiseshell

Jewelry and eyeglasses frames were once made of a flexible natural plastic created from turtle and tortoise shells.

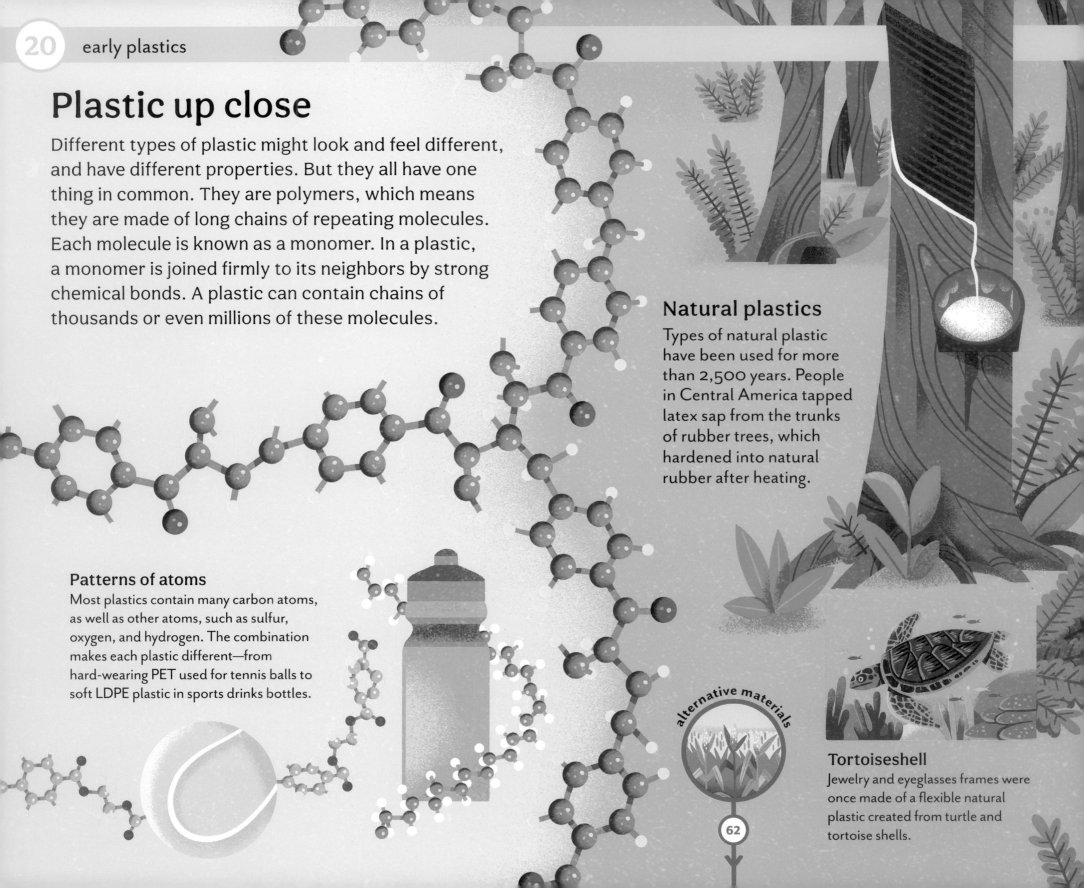

sticking around

9

Human-made plastics

In the 1800s, chemists started to experiment with making their own plastics. Artificial rubber was first created by chemists treating natural rubber with sulfur. The new material was used for bike tires and shoe soles.

Replacing natural plastics

Made from plant fibers, cellulose was one of the first plastics created as an alternative to natural plastics and animal ivory. It replaced these materials in rolls of movie film, piano keys, and dentures.

Synthetic plastics

The first completely synthetic plastic, made by chemical processes only, was Bakelite. It proved popular for everything from telephones to buttons.

Plastic connections

Natural plastics have a long history, but the plastics we are most familiar with are human-made and invented in the last 100 years. These synthetic plastics have proven wildly popular.

Animal horn

Combs, cutlery, and the windows in early lanterns were carved from the horn of certain animals. Cheaper materials are now used.

Shellac

Varnish and early vinyl records were made from the resin of female lac insects. Today, vinyl is made from synthetic plastic.

How plastics are made

More than 95 percent of plastics are made in a chemical process using fossil fuels, such as oil and natural gas. These substances are found deep underground and are extracted from the Earth through drilling or mining. They are then transported to refineries where they are processed and turned into a wide range of different plastics. The demand for plastic is rising fast—around twice as much is produced today as was made in 2000.

Plastic production

A distillation tower heats crude oil to turn it from a liquid into a vapor. The tower separates oil into substances known as fractions. Naphtha is the most commonly used fraction in plastic production.

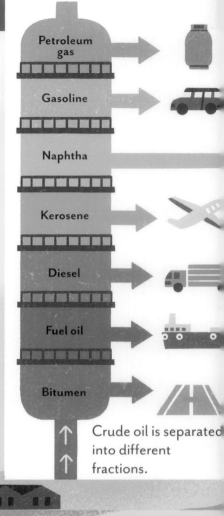

Petroleum gas

Gasoline

Naphtha

Kerosene

Diesel

Fuel oil

Bitumen

Crude oil is separated into different fractions.

Moving oil

Much crude oil and natural gas is obtained from wells drilled at sea. Crude oil extracted from the Earth is carried by giant tanker ships or a pipeline to oil refineries on land.

Where fossil fuels come from

Fossile fuels are natural fuels, such as coal and oil, found in Earth's crust. They are formed from decomposing plants and animals placed under pressure by layers of mud and rocks building up above them.

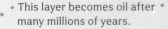

This layer becomes oil after many millions of years.

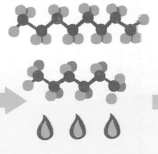

Naphtha is "cracked." It is broken down by heat into lighter substances, such as propylene and ethylene. These form the building blocks of many plastics.

Chemical reactions caused by heat and other substances create long polymer chains made up of smaller, repeating molecules.

Other substances can be added to make a particular type of plastic. Sometimes these are toxic and harmful. Chemical dyes can be mixed in to create a certain color.

Plastic connections

Most plastics are made from processing fossil fuels. The demand for plastic has increased and the way it is produced has improved. We are now making tens of millions of tons a year.

nurdles overboard

36

Liquid to solid

After processing, the liquid plastic is cooled to form a solid. It is then either crushed to make a powder or, more usually, chopped into small pieces called nurdles.

Nurdles are shipped in their trillions around the world to factories, which melt them in order to make plastic materials or products.

Plastic boom

Every year, so much new plastic is made that it would weigh about the same as 3.5 million blue whales. That's 450 million tons. In 1960, the world only produced around 8 million tons of new plastic each year.

why do we use plastic?

Plastic became popular in the 1950s. It was hailed as a wonder material that was cheap, light, and lasted well. Suddenly, things that had been made of wood, metals, or ceramics were made from plastic. Most homes today are packed with far more plastic than you realize.

popularity

Some of plastic's popularity is down to its price and the choice it offers. It often costs less to produce a plastic object than to use other materials, and it comes in every size and shape imaginable.

many uses

Plastic's useful properties mean it can be used for many different things—from molded cases to waterproof rainwear and see-through food wrap.

advantages

Most plastics are lightweight, cheap, and are easily shaped. These useful properties have made plastic extremely popular.

indoors

26

outdoors

27

light and cheap

28

many shapes

30

Inside and outdoors

When you get up tomorrow, count the number of plastic items you use and touch in the first half hour of your day. You may be surprised by how many there are. Even items you do not think of as plasticky, such as soft carpets and rugs or hard laminate flooring, may be made of plastic. Some homes are full of them!

Bathroom

Your bathroom contains a lot of plastic. From squeezy LDPE shampoo bottles and the nylon bristles of your toothbrush to modern bathtubs and shower trays, plastic is everywhere.

Many children's toys are made from ABS–a tough, glossy, solid plastic.

Computer

Between 20 and 40 percent of a computer is plastic. Inside, electronics are mounted on plastic circuit boards and linked by plastic-covered wiring.

Food may be carried in a reusable box or case made of washable polypropylene plastic.

Child's bedroom

Clothes, toys, and footwear are often plastic. Rubbery wheels and buttons in toys are usually made of polyvinyl chloride, or PVC. Much of your wardrobe will be filled with clothes made of polyester, acrylic, or nylon—all types of plastic.

any shape

31

Outdoors
From this balcony, you can see UPVC window frames, weather-resistant balcony furniture made from ASA plastic, and a tough plastic bicycle helmet lined with polystyrene foam.

Plastic connections
Plastics are low-cost and adaptable materials. As a result, many modern homes are filled with objects made partly or wholly of plastic.

Kitchen cupboards contain many PET plastic bottles, jars, and other food containers.

Plastic can even be found in stout fridge doors.

Living room
Plastic fibers woven into carpets make them more hard-wearing. Beneath some carpets are spongey layers made of polyurethane foams. The same plastic is found inside sofas and chairs to provide cushioning.

Kitchen
From thin LDPE shopping, freezer, and bin bags to kitchen worktops made of strong, rigid polycarbonate, plastic is everywhere in the kitchen. Cooking utensils are often made of heat-resistant plastics.

Light, tough, and cheap

Plastic is tough, hard-wearing, and widely used in hospitals, at work, and in the home. It can also make products much lighter in weight. A small plastic drink bottle weighs a tenth of a similar-sized glass bottle. But the biggest appeal of plastic is cost. It is often far cheaper to make bags, packaging, and product parts from plastic than any other material.

Good for medicine

Plastic has become useful in medicine for syringes, masks, gloves, and bandages. This is because they are cheap and can be disposed of easily. Throwing the plastic items away reduces the risk of germs spreading.

single-use bags

10

Bubble wrap

This type of packaging contains pockets of air trapped between thin layers of plastic. It offers lightweight protection for delicate objects.

Light

Plastic is used in parcels and packaging because it is very lightweight. The lighter the item and its packaging, the less fuel needed for its delivery.

Saving weight

Fuel for planes is costly and harms the environment. Lighter ones need less fuel to fly. Modern planes use lots of plastic parts to save weight.

essential plastics

54

Tough

Some plastics save lives. They can be made tough and shatterproof for use in motorcycle helmets and other safety equipment.

Vehicle parts

A third of a lorry is made of plastic, from the bumpers to the controls. This is because plastic parts are lighter than most other materials.

Cheap

Low-cost plastics like polystyrene can be molded into different shapes. They are used to protect expensive items such as computers and televisions.

Packing peanuts

Small, squeezy pieces of Styrofoam plastic fill up space around expensive or delicate objects. They cushion and protect, absorbing shocks as boxes are bumped around.

Plastic connections

Plastics have many useful properties. They protect objects and people, and their cheapness and light weight makes things easier to transport.

Easily shaped

Compared to many materials, plastic is very adaptable. It can be worked into almost any shape or object. Millions of plastic straws, pipes, and tubes are created every day by a process called extrusion, for example. This is where soft plastic is squeezed by machine through nozzles to form long strands. Extrusion is just one of many different shaping processes possible with plastic.

Thin sheets

Slim plastic sheets, such as shower curtains and PVC clothing, are made by squeezing heated soft plastic between heavy rollers, or calenders.

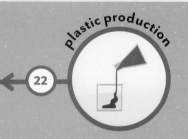

plastic production

← 22

Thermoplastics

These are plastics that soften when heated and harden when cool. They can be shaped and formed, reheated many times, and are usually recyclable.

Molded shapes

Plastic bicycle helmets, yogurt trays, and bathtubs are made from a process called vacuum forming. A plastic sheet is heated until soft and placed over a mold. All the air is then removed, which sucks the sheet around the mold.

Hollow plastics

Blow molding is used to make plant pots, bottles, and other hollow plastic objects. Liquid plastic or soft plastic passes into a mold. Air is then blown in to force the plastic to cling to the sides of the mold, forming the chosen shape.

Plastic fibers

Some clothing fibers are actually plastic. Plastic is forced through a sievelike device containing lots of tiny holes, creating the fibers.

microfibres 37

Hard plastics

The most common form of molding is when liquid plastic is injected under pressure into a mold. It is used to make model kits, toys, and cases for hair dryers and other electrical items.

3D printing

A 3D printed plastic is made from hundreds or thousands of layers. A nozzle deposits thin layers of heated plastic wire until they eventually build up to form an object.

Liquid plastics

Some plastics are kept as a liquid. They are mixed in with other substances to form liquid paints or glues.

Industrial plastics

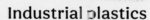

Strong plastics, such as pot and pan handles, bowls, and car parts, are created by compression molding. This is where plastic granules are heated and pressed in a mold.

Plastic connections

Plastics can be shaped, molded, and formed in many different ways. This makes them a popular choice of material and is why so many plastic products are being produced.

why is
plastic in the
ocean?

Since production began, more than 9 billion tons of plastic have been made. It may be produced on land, yet most plastic eventually finds its way into the sea. At least 8 million tons enter the world's oceans every single year!

plastic ocean

Up to one-fifth of all the plastic in the ocean has been dumped or lost at sea. The rest enters the ocean via the world's many streams and rivers.

natural transport

Wind, rain, and water runoff from land carry lightweight plastics into rivers and streams. Rivers empty the plastic waste they carry as they flow into the ocean.

human activity

Plastic waste is littered, dumped, and thrown away in drains and sewers. The same happens on the ocean. This leads to a buildup of plastic in the sea.

sewers

34

waterways

35

making microplastics

36

dumping

38

litter

39

Traveling out to sea

Much of the plastic in the ocean gets there via the world's rivers and streams. These networks of waterways flow downward from higher land to lower areas before finally emptying into the ocean. Litter and plastic dumped on land are often transported by wind and rain into waterways or drains, which then flow into rivers or directly out to sea.

Blown away
Most plastic litter is very lightweight and can easily be blown long distances, often into water sources.

Down the drain

Wet wipes, disposable diapers, and other plastic waste flushed down toilets enter sewage systems. These may cause blockages or take time and energy to filter out at sewage plants. In some places, wastewater including plastics is pumped directly into the ocean.

microplastics

36

Flowing through filters
Some plastic particles are small enough to pass through sewage-system filters and flow out with the water into the sea.

dumping

38

Dumping and accidents

Old fishing lines, nets, and baskets may be deliberately dumped at sea. Other plastic gets there by accident, such as when a boat capsizes or cargo containers of plastic goods fall overboard.

Coastal litter

Plastic cups, bags, toys, and cutlery left as litter on beaches and coastlines are frequently blown or washed out to sea.

Plastic connections

Plastic in the ocean is a problem that begins on land. Most plastic objects are light and can float, so water can carry them long distances. We must be careful with our plastic production and use so it does not end up in the sea.

Go with the flow

Waterways are connected and flow into one another. This means that plastic waste dumped or dropped in one location can easily travel hundreds of miles and be carried out to sea.

Creating microplastics

They may be small, but microplastics are creating big problems. These tiny pieces of plastic are just a quarter-inch or less in size, and are littering our ocean in their trillions. Microplastics can turn seawater cloudy and stop underwater plants and plankton from getting the sunlight they need to grow. They can also clog the insides of marine creatures. Microplastics form and reach the ocean in many different ways.

Rubber ruin
Vehicle tires wear away on roads, producing tiny fragments. Some of these get washed down drains or into rivers, and can end up flowing out to sea.

Nurdles overboard
Small pellets of plastic are used by factories and might be dumped as waste or fall into the sea by accident. Ships have been known to collide and as a result deposit many tons of nurdles into the ocean.

accidents

35

Polystyrene
Cups and packaging made from polystyrene break down into small pieces easily. They may be blown or washed into rivers and seas.

plastic-free washing   59

Microbeads

Tiny plastic beads can be found in toothpaste, cosmetics, and sunscreens in some countries. When washed away, they enter the ocean via sewer systems.

Microfibers

Thousands of microscopic fibers from plastic fabrics are shed every time they are washed. Thinner than a human hair, some microfibers pass through washing machines and sewage-treatment filters to end up in the ocean.

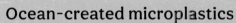

Ocean-created microplastics

Larger pieces of plastic in the ocean become brittle in sunlight. As these are bumped and bashed by ocean waves, they break down. Over time, the pieces get smaller and smaller, eventually forming microplastics.

Plastic connections

Microplastics are formed in many ways. Most occur due to wear and tear. Their small size makes it hard to stop them reaching the ocean.

Shoreline to seafloor

Not all ocean plastics are found floating on the surface. A lot is washed up onto beaches and shorelines, where it is smelly, ugly, and potentially harmful. Plastic also drops deep below the surface and can be hard to detect. This may mean that the problem of plastic waste in the ocean is even bigger than scientists think.

ocean microplastics

37

Plastic overboard

Hundreds of thousands of ships and boats sail the seas catching fish and seafood. They often lose, abandon, or dump overboard broken plastic nets, ropes, traps, and baskets. This is called ghost gear, and it litters the ocean.

Out at sea

In the open ocean, microplastics and larger plastic items can form layers of waste at different depths. Some lie many feet below the surface and can be hard to locate and measure.

Deepest dive

Submersibles, or underwater craft, have even found plastic bags, candy wrappers, and other waste items at Challenger Deep, the deepest point in the world's oceans.

Deep down

Some plastic is heavy and dense enough to sink to the ocean floor. There it can entangle and harm marine plants and creatures.

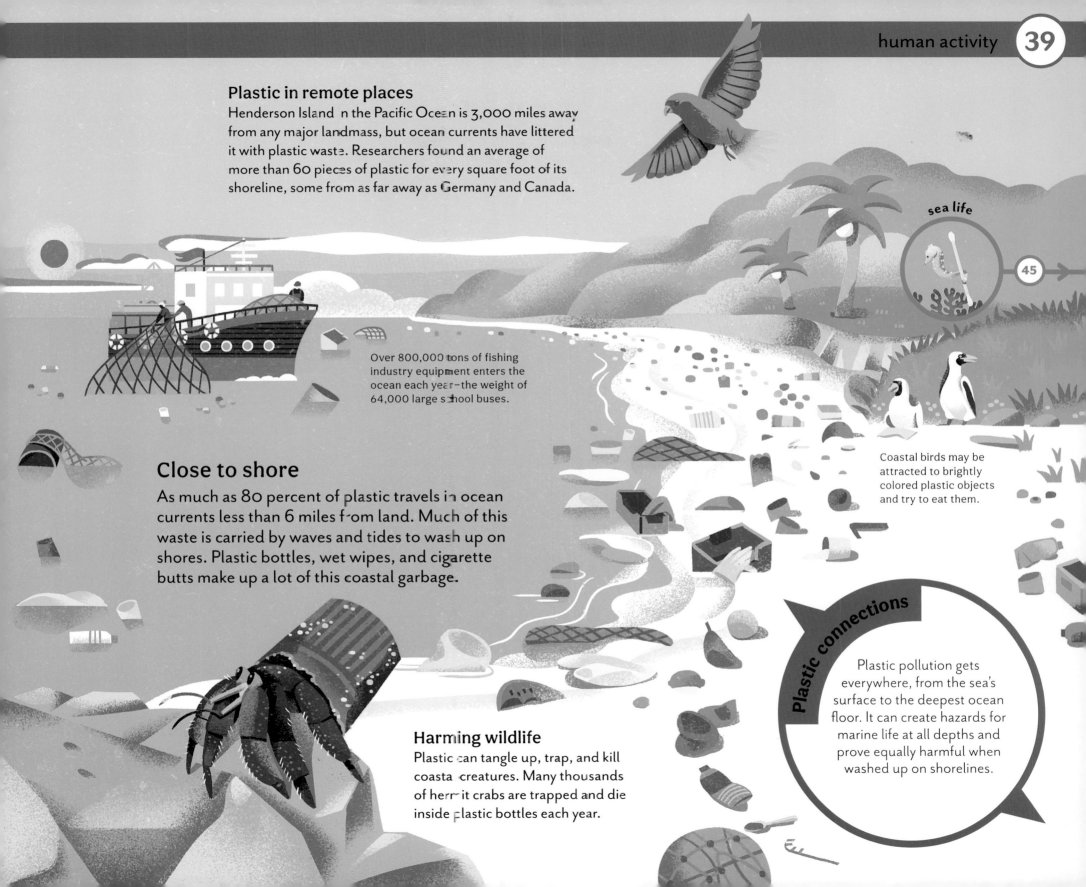

Plastic in remote places

Henderson Island in the Pacific Ocean is 3,000 miles away from any major landmass, but ocean currents have littered it with plastic waste. Researchers found an average of more than 60 pieces of plastic for every square foot of its shoreline, some from as far away as Germany and Canada.

sea life

45

Over 800,000 tons of fishing industry equipment enters the ocean each year—the weight of 64,000 large school buses.

Close to shore

As much as 80 percent of plastic travels in ocean currents less than 6 miles from land. Much of this waste is carried by waves and tides to wash up on shores. Plastic bottles, wet wipes, and cigarette butts make up a lot of this coastal garbage.

Coastal birds may be attracted to brightly colored plastic objects and try to eat them.

Harming wildlife

Plastic can tangle up, trap, and kill coastal creatures. Many thousands of hermit crabs are trapped and die inside plastic bottles each year.

Plastic connections

Plastic pollution gets everywhere, from the sea's surface to the deepest ocean floor. It can create hazards for marine life at all depths and prove equally harmful when washed up on shorelines.

is plastic
harming the
ocean?

Scientists are still learning about the effects of plastic in the ocean. But it is clear that it causes pollution and damages habitats. They are also getting a better idea of how much plastic is being taken into creatures' bodies, and what harm it might do to food chains.

pollution

Plastics, big and small, pollute ocean waters, the seabed, and coral reefs. They cause problems in all of these places.

garbage patches

42

ocean habitats

44

ocean harm

Many sea creatures, and nearly half of all seabirds, have plastic in their bodies. Larger floating plastic waste is easy to spot and avoid, but the mounting trillions of near-invisible microplastic pieces are easy to swallow.

food chain

Plastic travels through and disrupts food chains. This harms food supplies and many marine creatures in the process.

marine life

46

humans

47

Connecting currents

The world's oceans cover almost 70 percent of the Earth's surface. There are five of them—the Pacific, Atlantic, Indian, Arctic, and Southern. But in reality, they all form one big, connected system. Large paths of moving water, or currents, transport seawater so that it flows between the oceans. This means that plastic waste entering one ocean can end up almost anywhere in the world.

out to sea

Old plastic
The Great Pacific Garbage Patch was thought to be a recent phenomenon. But plastic crates from more than 50 years ago have since been found among its waste.

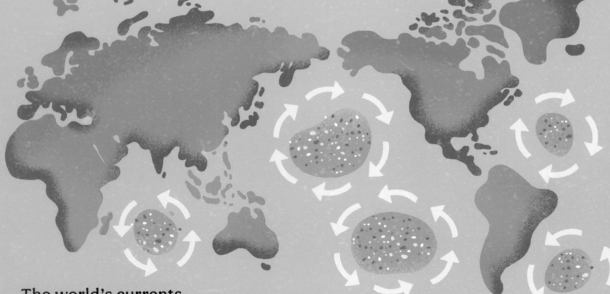

The world's currents
Circular ocean currents called gyres are caused by Earth's rotation and the planet's winds. There are five major gyres. Pieces of plastic waste get caught up in the swirling gyres and often gather in their calm centers, forming garbage patches.

Plastic garbage patches
Lying between Hawaii and the US coast is the Great Pacific Garbage Patch. This area of plastic is up to three times the size of France, although it is hard to measure exactly due to many of its billions of plastic pieces lying below the surface.

Discovered by accident

The Great Pacific Garbage Patch was discovered by a yachtsman in 1997. Research shows it is growing as more plastic is dumped in the ocean.

Plastic islands

In places within a garbage patch, discarded fishing nets, bottles, and other large plastic objects form tangled, floating islands of garbage. It often smells bad due to algae growing on the waste.

Washed overboard

During a storm in 1992, a container of nearly 30,000 plastic bath toys fell off a Pacific Ocean cargo ship. Plastic ducks, turtles, and frogs ended up on the coasts of Australia, Alaska, Europe, and South America. This demonstrates just how far ocean currents can carry things.

plastic in sealife

Plastic soup

Most of an ocean garbage patch is made up of billions of pieces of tiny microplastics suspended in the water. They form a cloudy, soupy mess.

46

Plastic connections

Plastic pollution is spread all around the world by the interconnected oceans and their currents. The large size of ocean garbage patches highlights how much plastic is polluting the sea.

Sea life

The planet's oceans are a treasure trove of extraordinary living things, especially shallow water regions containing coral reefs. These rich habitats cover less than 1 percent of the world's oceans yet are home to around 20 percent of all ocean life. Now reefs and other parts of the ocean are under threat from plastic waste. More than a million fish each year are killed by plastic, which has partly caused seabird numbers to fall by two-thirds since 1950.

A flesh-footed shearwater carries deadly plastic to her nest to feed her chicks.

False food
Seabirds may mistake floating plastic granules for fish eggs or colored plastic for small fish. Once swallowed, sharp plastics can wound a bird's organs or fill their stomachs up. Most seabirds now have plastic in their stomachs.

Algal attraction
Algae growing on plastics that have been in the ocean a long time gives off similar scents to fish and birds' normal food. Both the algae and plastic may be eaten up by hungry creatures.

Deadly bait
Some fish get trapped in plastic waste and are unable to swim free. Many more perish due to plastic clogging their mouths, gills, and stomachs, stopping them from breathing and eating.

plastic in seafood

47

Wounding coral
Plastics block out the sunlight that corals need to flourish. Hard plastics can damage corals' outer surface. Their wounds may get infected, especially as some plastics carry harmful bacteria.

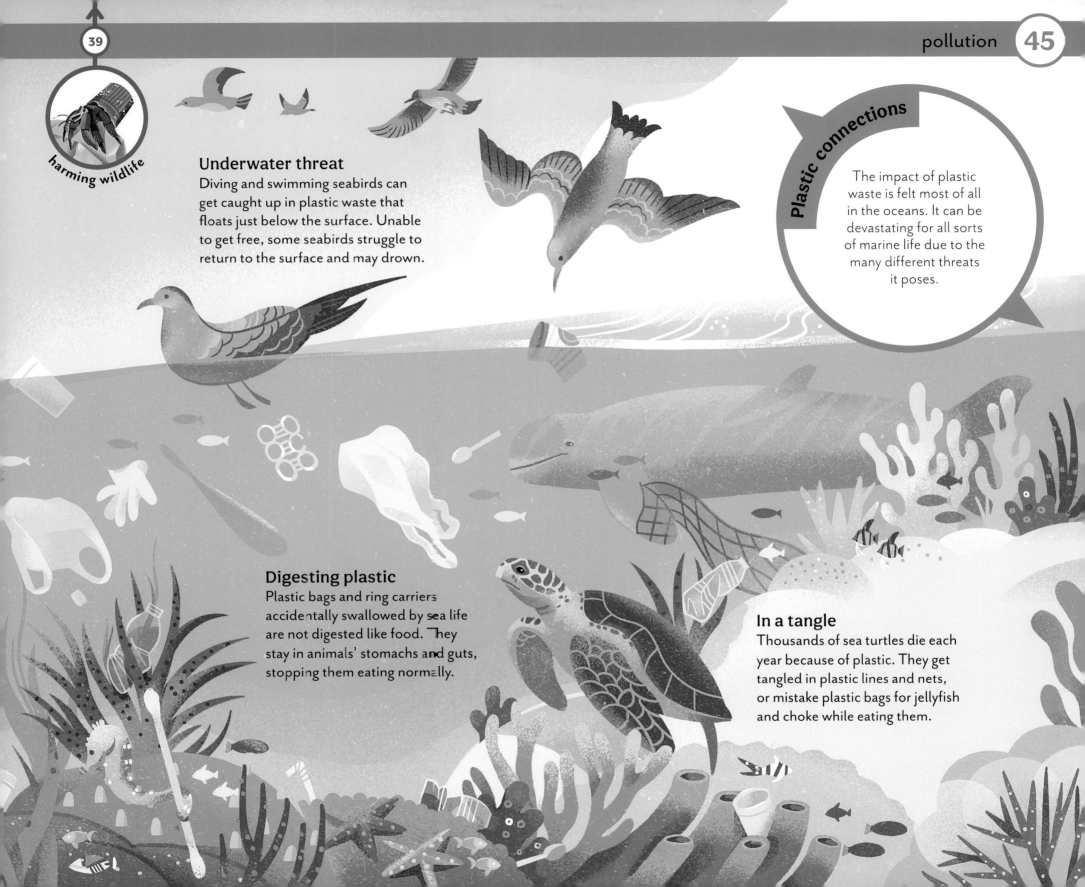

harming wildlife

Underwater threat
Diving and swimming seabirds can get caught up in plastic waste that floats just below the surface. Unable to get free, some seabirds struggle to return to the surface and may drown.

Plastic connections
The impact of plastic waste is felt most of all in the oceans. It can be devastating for all sorts of marine life due to the many different threats it poses.

Digesting plastic
Plastic bags and ring carriers accidentally swallowed by sea life are not digested like food. They stay in animals' stomachs and guts, stopping them eating normally.

In a tangle
Thousands of sea turtles die each year because of plastic. They get tangled in plastic lines and nets, or mistake plastic bags for jellyfish and choke while eating them.

Microplastic food chains

The average person eats at least 50,000 pieces of microplastic a year, and breathes in even more. A lot of it comes from eating animals that have consumed microplastics. Some of this plastic can build up in our bodies. Scientists are investigating what harm microplastics inside us might cause. Many experts think they could damage cells and affect breathing and how our bodies fight disease. Chemicals from plastics may even affect growth.

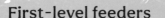

zooplankton

First-level feeders
Tiny zooplankton exist in their trillions, and are the first level of feeder animals in the ocean food chain. They take in microplastic fibers with the water they absorb when feeding on plant plankton.

krill

mackerel eat krill and the plastic inside them

tuna

Second-level feeders
First-level feeders are eaten by larger fish, such as shrimplike creatures called krill. Plastic inside the animals passes along the food chain.

Ocean food chain

A food chain describes how living things feed on other living things. This gives them the energy and nutrients they need to survive. Food chains usually start with plants, which make their own food. When an animal eats a plant or other animal, energy is passed along the food chain. Each living thing is a link in a food chain.

Higher-level feeders
Creatures that hunt may also be hunted. Mackerel are eaten by tuna fish, which are themselves caught by people to eat.

cleaning the seas

51

microplastics

Seafood

When we eat seafood, we are likely to eat microplastics, too. It is thought that up to three-quarters of fish may now contain microplastics.

Plastic water

Tiny plastic particles have been found in bottled water and tap water. Most microplastics are so small that our eyes cannot spot them.

Salt

When you sprinkle salt over your food, you may also be adding microplastics to your plate. Microplastics have been found in many types of sea salt. Most sea salt is made by evaporating seawater, leaving behind salt and any microplastics from the water.

Plastic connections

As ocean creatures eat other living things, microplastics can be passed along food chains to reach people. Plastic may build up in our bodies and release chemicals that might restrict growth or cause harm.

how do we
start to
clear up?

We need to build a future that relies far less on plastic. But before we get there, we also have to deal with the mess plastic has made on land and in the oceans. Action is needed to clean up the damage already done and to start reducing the amount of plastic we use now.

less plastic

Reducing the amount of plastic on our planet is a big challenge. It needs people, communities, and countries to work together to clean up plastic waste and make big choices that mean we all use less plastic.

clearing it up

The plastic waste already polluting our planet needs to be cleared up. Charities, communities, and scientists are working together to help.

less new plastic

New plastics can be reduced through bans and new laws. Countries can encourage changes in buying habits and support alternatives to plastic.

cleanups

50

technology

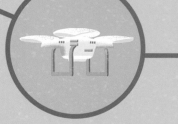

52

new laws

54

bans and taxes

55

Cleaning up

Plastic pollution gets everywhere, from bags stuck in trees to microplastics found inside food. It often travels a long way from where it was first dumped. Cleaning plastic waste from somewhere can take a lot of time and effort, but many people feel it is worth it. Cleanups can make places more attractive and less dangerous for the people and creatures there.

Who pays?
Many people think that governments and the companies who produce plastics the most should pay to clean them up.

Waste collectors
Most cleanups are done by people who collect and sort waste to earn money, volunteers giving up their free time, and recycling companies. Their actions help make public spaces plastic-free.

litter picks

Picking up plastics
People, charities, schools, or whole communities can organize cleanup events in their local area. All they need are safety gloves, bags, and litter-picking tools.

68

PET

PET, or polyethylene terephthalate, bottles are among the most common items picked at cleanups.

coastal litter

Using drones

Some flying drones are being taught to recognize and map where plastic pollution occurs. Their cameras identify different types of plastic waste.

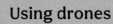

On the water

Boats, kayaks, and rafts allow volunteers to fish out plastic floating in rivers, streams, and lakes. Some waterways are fitted with long booms and nets called traps to guide plastic waste into one place for easier collection.

Clean coasts

Many groups pick litter up from beaches and coastlines. The Ocean Conservancy helps organize thousands of International Coastal Cleanup events every year. Around a million people take part, collecting and sorting waste into different types of plastic or plastic products.

Plastic connections

Plastic is polluting our land and oceans. By cleaning up our surroundings and reducing plastic waste, we can help create a healthier place to live.

HDPE

High-density polyethylene, or HDPE, items gathered during cleanups can often be sent for recycling.

PP

Bottle caps and food packaging made of polypropylene, or PP, are frequently found.

Collecting and recording

The information logged by groups cleaning up the coasts is useful to scientists researching plastic pollution. It helps give them a clearer picture of the size of the problem.

Science and technology

Engineers and scientists are working hard to develop new chemistry and technology that will help tackle the plastic problem. Some are building machines that can remove plastic waste from rivers, seas, and coasts. Others are trying to find ways of making plastics easier to recycle or be removed from the environment. If these work well, they could have a positive impact.

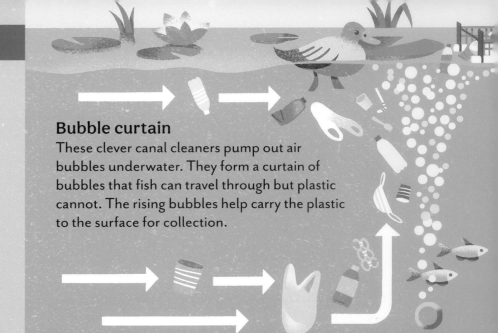

Bubble curtain

These clever canal cleaners pump out air bubbles underwater. They form a curtain of bubbles that fish can travel through but plastic cannot. The rising bubbles help carry the plastic to the surface for collection.

River cleaners

Robotic machines have been designed to cruise rivers, scooping up litter floating on or near the water's surface. Some can gather more than 1,000 pounds of trash, much of it plastic, in one day.

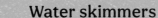

new ideas

67

Water skimmers

Special boats gather in plastic garbage from rivers, lakes, coasts, and oceans. They carry the plastic waste by conveyor belt into big sacks for disposal.

Plastic-eating bacteria

Some bacteria and fungi produce special chemicals that break down plastics such as PET. Scientists are studying ways these chemicals might tackle river or ocean pollution in the future.

Rotting plastics away

Chemists are experimenting with adding chemicals to existing plastics. These might make plastics rot away far more quickly once they are thrown away, reducing the plastic waste problem.

drones

Sand sucker

A special vacuum cleaner worn as a backpack can suck up sand from a beach and filter out the plastic in it. It can gather more than a million microplastic pieces in a few hours.

Boats visit regularly to carry the plastic waste away for disposal.

The boom moves slowly, stopping plastic from drifting away.

Ocean clean-up

Invented by a Dutch teenager, this 2,000-foot-long, C-shaped boom floats in ocean garbage patches. As it moves on ocean currents, it gathers up lots of floating plastic.

Plastic connections

Science and technology can help clean up, but they cannot solve the entire plastic problem. We also need to move away from producing so much plastic in the first place.

Banning plastics

If plastics are so harmful, why do countries not ban them? It is not always that simple. Plastics are popular with companies and people for many reasons, especially their light weight and low cost. Some are considered essential and other materials will not do as good a job. A ban on all plastic is unlikely, but many countries are banning or restricting the sale or use of some plastics, particularly single-use products.

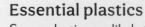

Essential plastics

Some plastics are likely to remain in use because they increase safety, like in shock-absorbing helmets. Plastics are used in medical supplies, as they can be thrown away safely.

Some campaigners are asking for a limit on the amount of new plastic companies are allowed to make.

Saying no to plastic

Campaigns let people know about the problems with plastic. They can encourage governments or companies to redesign products with less plastic.

single-use

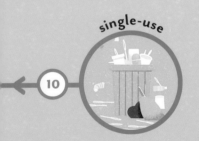

Making things affordable

Plastic is often the cheapest material to make things with. Using alternatives to plastic can increase the prices of goods, which many people cannot afford. Ways must be found to make alternative materials cheaper.

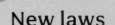

New laws

Some countries have banned certain plastic items, such as straws, food trays, and containers. More than 90 nations have introduced laws banning single-use plastic bags.

Global agreement

The United Nations has agreed to produce a worldwide treaty on plastic pollution. All nations must promise they will carefully check where and how plastic is used in their country.

Selling less plastic

Supermarkets can do more to get rid of plastic. They can sell food in reusable packaging, or let shoppers bring their own containers to refill drinks, pasta, shampoo, and other products.

Plastic connections

Countries and companies have the power to reduce global plastic use in a big way. Bans and taxes on some plastic items are just some of the ways in which they can fight plastic pollution.

Different packaging

Some companies are exploring using less or no plastic in their packaging. They are replacing plastic with card and paper or gluing cans together instead of using plastic ring carriers.

Banning wrapping

A handful of countries have banned plastic wrapping from covering individual fruit and vegetables. Supermarkets in some nations offer plastic-free aisles of unwrapped goods.

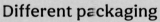

use your own bags

Taxing plastics

Since the 1990s, many countries have launched a tax on plastic bags. Making people pay for throwaway plastic items reduces the numbers used.

can we stop using plastic?

Plastic is now part of so many things that we buy, use, and throw away. We are so used to plastic that it can be hard to remember there are other options. But there are plenty of alternatives if you look out for them.

stop plastic

Companies will only make and sell plastic while people want to buy it. Choosing plastic-free options will push companies to change what they make, and help stop new plastic being produced.

use less

Choose nonplastic options when possible. Reuse and recycle far more of the remaining plastics to keep them out of the garbage can.

reuse, repair

58

avoid

59

recycle

60

materials

Alternatives to plastic can be used far more. We must also find ways of living that need fewer new plastic materials in the first place.

traditional

62

alternatives

63

A less plastic life

There is lots you can do every day to reduce your plastic use and waste. Sometimes it is just making the choice not to buy something new, and making do and repairing what you already have. At other times, it may mean avoiding packaging or throwaway plastics such as straws and bags. Even choosing objects with less plastic over others with more will help. It is amazing how much new plastic you can avoid with just a little thought and effort.

Avoid plastic clothes

Many new clothes contain plastic. Try to buy fewer new clothes and avoid wearing something just a few times before throwing it away. Instead, wear your clothes for longer, swap items with friends, or get them secondhand from thrift stores.

different packaging 55

Reusing plastic bottles and containers is a clever way to avoid new plastic.

Reuse

Reduce your plastic waste by choosing reusable items instead of single-use plastics. Drinking from a refillable bottle avoids plastic bottles being bought, used once, and then thrown away.

Reworking plastic

Old plastics heading for the trash can get a second life by being turned into useful objects. Try making them into bird feeders, jewelry or pencil holders.

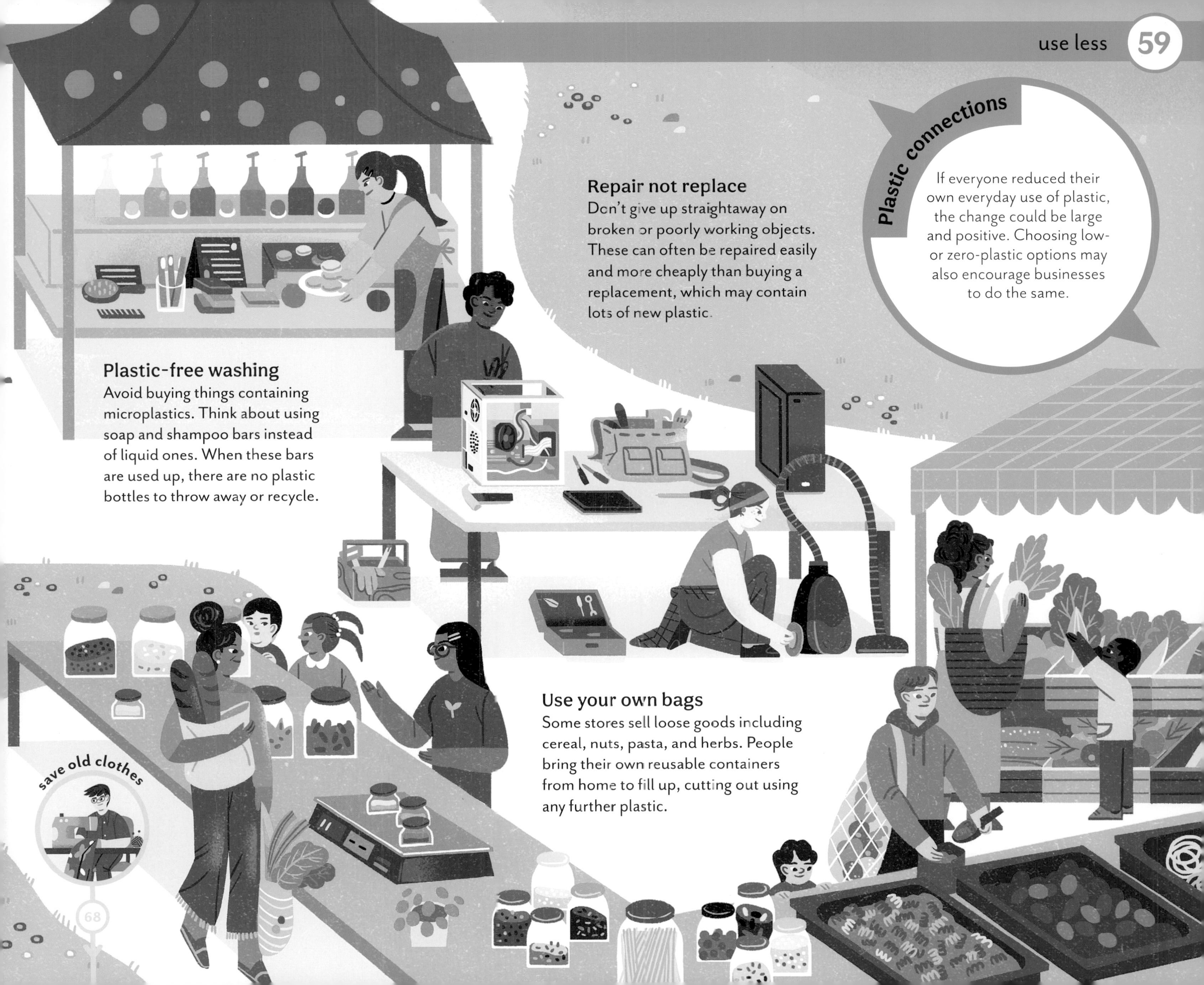

Plastic connections

If everyone reduced their own everyday use of plastic, the change could be large and positive. Choosing low- or zero-plastic options may also encourage businesses to do the same.

Repair not replace

Don't give up straightaway on broken or poorly working objects. These can often be repaired easily and more cheaply than buying a replacement, which may contain lots of new plastic.

Plastic-free washing

Avoid buying things containing microplastics. Think about using soap and shampoo bars instead of liquid ones. When these bars are used up, there are no plastic bottles to throw away or recycle.

Use your own bags

Some stores sell loose goods including cereal, nuts, pasta, and herbs. People bring their own reusable containers from home to fill up, cutting out using any further plastic.

save old clothes

68

Recycling

If you cannot repair or reuse plastic, the next best thing you can do is to recycle it properly. Recycling plastic stops some energy and resources from going into new plastic. Importantly, it also avoids unwanted plastic waste from entering landfill or being dumped on land or in the oceans. Only nine percent of all the plastic ever made has been recycled. While recycling plastic is complicated and takes time and energy, it is worth it to avoid making new plastic.

repair and reuse

Plastic waste
The plastic recycling process often starts when waste is picked up by garbage trucks. It is then carried away to a recycling center.

Separating waste
Start recycling by sorting through your waste. Place unwanted plastics in the correct recycling bins found at school or at home, ready for collection.

Types of plastic
Plastic items are marked with a number inside a triangle. These tell recycling centers what sort of plastic it is and whether it can be recycled.

01 – PET
Drinks bottles, food-to-go trays

02 – HDPE
Milk jugs, bags, shampoo bottles

03 – PVC
Tubing, pipes, blister packs for tablets

04 – LDPE
Squeezable bottles, shrink wrap, bags

05 – PP
Bottle caps, toys, straws

06 – PS
Packaging, hot-drink cups, packing peanuts

07 – O
CDs, acrylic clothing, nylon toothbrushes

Some plastics are not usually recycled. They are more likely to go to landfill.

Sorting
Plastics are sorted at a recycling center. Different plastic types are sorted into separate streams.

recycle at home

69

Shredding
The plastic is shredded or ground down by machine into smaller pieces, which pass along a conveyor belt.

Melted down
The plastic is heated and melts. It is then formed into nurdles. These pellets can be shipped to factories making new plastic products.

Washed and dried
Water jets and driers clean the shredded plastic. Further sorting may remove any unsuitable materials.

New plastic
Plastic is often recycled into different objects. This is because plastic's molecules are slightly damaged by recycling, so the new plastic is not of a good enough quality to be used in the same way as before.

PET
PET plastic is often recycled into rucksacks, or carpet or fabric fibers.

HDPE
HDPE plastic can be recycled into outdoor toys and plant pots.

Plastic connections
Recycling can give plastic a new life. Not all plastic can be recycled, so we must be careful about the types of plastic we buy. If plastic cannot be avoided or reused, then the next best thing we can do is recycle it!

Alternative materials

Material scientists are hard at work tackling the plastic problem. Some are trying to develop new, less harmful alternatives to plastics made with fossil fuels. Others are looking into using existing materials in new ways to replace plastics. Scientists have found that crushed oats or walnut shells are a substitute for plastic microbeads in facial scrubs. But no alternative is perfect. All have their own problems as well as benefits.

Bamboo
Grasses such as bamboo are fast growers. A few types can grow 20 inches a day and end up more than 60 feet tall. Strands from their stems can make socks and toothbrush bristles, and replace plastic cotton swabs and straws.

different packaging

55

Card and paper
It takes more energy and water to make cardboard than plastic packaging. But unlike plastic, card biodegrades quickly and is more easily recycled. New trees can also be grown to keep making more card and paper. Oil for plastic will one day run out.

Aluminum
A lightweight metal, aluminum is mined from rocks and used to make foil, cans, and containers. It can replace some plastic containers and can be recycled many times, but takes lots of energy to make.

Cornstarch plastic

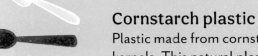

Plastic made from cornstarch comes from corn kernels. This natural plastic has been turned into bin liners, dog waste bags, and throwaway crockery and cutlery. It can replace some single-use plastics, but only rots away easily in particular conditions.

11

single-use cups

Seaweed

There are millions of tons of seaweed in Earth's oceans. Some is being turned into a different material for single-use cups and food packets. Seaweed packaging is far more expensive than plastic at the moment, but it does biodegrade in weeks rather than centuries.

Casein plastic

A natural plastic called casein was first made from cow's milk in the 1900s. Scientists are now trying to develop less fragile versions that are easier to make. It could replace the plastic in many food and drinks containers. Casein rots quite quickly once it is thrown away.

Plastic connections

Many alternatives to plastic exist or are being developed. While some biodegrade far more quickly than plastic, more work needs to be done to make them less expensive to manufacture.

what
else can
we do?

The plastic problem can seem huge and overwhelming at times, but everyone can play a part in tackling the harm it is causing. It is not too late to take action. By working together, every single person can help clean up the plastic mess, reduce its use and protect our planet.

next steps

Countries, communities, and individuals all have a responsibility to take action to solve the plastic problem. There are many different ways we can all play a part.

working together

Groups of people, small and large, can call for change, make new laws, and find ways to reduce plastic use and waste.

people

66

companies

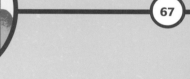

66

governments

67

every single person

Buy, use, and throw away less plastic every day. These and many other simple actions may seem small, but they all add up. You can make a difference.

swap, mend

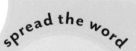

68

spread the word

69

packaging

69

What can we all do?

People worried about the plastic problem can use their voice to call for change. This can be on their own or as part of a group. Some groups focus on cleaning up their local area or offer alternatives to plastic. Others try to encourage a less plastic-based lifestyle. People can also try to talk to leaders in big companies and governments. It may make them change how they use plastic or create new laws to reduce plastic use.

Making the switch
All organizations can make simple yet positive changes. They can reduce plastic packaging or switch from plastic-based materials to bamboo and paper ones.

Changing minds
Many groups campaign to try to change people's minds. They want to make people more aware of the problems and the ways they can be solved.

say no to plastic

54

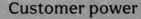

Customer power
When enough people protested, some fast-food companies stopped giving away plastic toys with children's meals. If enough people make their voices heard, companies may listen and change their ways.

Plastic connections

Working with other groups makes it easier to tackle the plastic problem. When enough people make themselves heard, leaders may realize they need to make changes to reduce plastic use.

Working with governments

Spreading the word about plastic can help governments work with people to take action. It may help them agree to better recycling, reducing or banning some plastic items, and controlling harmful chemicals in plastics.

New ideas

In some places, vending machines accept old plastic bottles for recycling. People are given a small amount of money for every bottle they put in the machine. This is one of the ideas governments can introduce to encourage people not to buy new plastic.

Writing in

If people feel strongly about an issue, they can join together with others to write a group letter. This lets governments and companies know that people want them to take action on plastics.

Children making change

Many successful protests have been started by children. Some have inspired others to do more recycling, avoid using plastic, or organize cleanup days. Other child protestors have made governments decide to change laws on plastics use.

What can you do?

You can play an important part in reducing the plastic on our planet. There are dozens of simple things you can do every day, from thinking about what you buy and what you eat to saying no to single-use plastics and writing to local or national leaders. On their own, these actions may seem small, but when large numbers of people do them, they can make a big difference. Encourage others to join in and make a change together!

Swap shop
Instead of throwing away plastic things you don't use anymore, set up a stall to swap them with other people. This stops them from going into landfill and helps avoid buying new plastic.

Save old clothes
Mend old clothes or alter them to fit you again. Recycle unwanted clothes by taking them to thrift stores. You could also swap clothes with others or buy them secondhand to avoid buying new items.

Clean up
Join a group that collects and cleans up the plastic garbage that litters a stream, pond, or park, and causes harm to wildlife. You could even set up a cleanup event with people in your school or local community.

Spread the word

Learn more about plastic problems and how you can help. After, share your knowledge with as many people as possible. Tell people where their plastic comes from and what happens to it.

Recycle

Ask your family to reduce plastic waste and improve their recycling. Make sure plastic objects are empty, clean, and dry before they go into the recycling bin. Don't forget to check plastic packaging so you know how it should be recycled.

Wrapping up

Don't buy and use plastic-based wrapping paper. Wrap presents in reused paper or interesting pages of newspapers or magazines.

Reduce food packaging

Reuse plastic containers with sealed lids for your lunches. Refill the same drink bottle rather than buying new cartons or bottles.

Plastic connections

We must all take steps to reduce our plastic use if we are to solve the plastic problem. Being aware of the plastic you use, reusing as much as you can, and avoiding single-use plastics are just some of the ways you can help.

Glossary

ABS Acrylonitrile butadiene styrene, which is used to make hard plastics.

acrylic A plastic that can be made into see-through sheets, molded into objects, or turned into fabric.

ASA Acrylonitrile styrene acrylate, a strong, tough plastic.

atom Tiny particles that are the building blocks of everything.

bacteria Tiny living things made of a single cell. Most bacteria cannot be seen without a microscope.

Bakelite One of the first human-made plastics.

biodegrading A process in which natural materials decay into simpler substances.

blow molding A method used in factories to make hollow plastic objects such as bottles.

climate change The ongoing changes to the world's climate.

compression molding A process using heat and pressure to shape plastic objects inside a mold.

crude oil Oil found in its natural state before it has been refined and processed.

decomposer A living thing, such as bacteria or fungi, that helps break down dead plant and animal material.

distillation tower A tall tower used at an oil refinery to separate the different parts of oil.

ecosystem A community of living things that depend on each other and their environment in many ways.

extraction The process of removing crude oil from the ground.

extrusion A way of making plastic rods or tubes by forcing plastic through a metal nozzle.

food chain A series of living things that depend on one another for food.

fossil fuel An energy-containing fuel, such as coal, oil, or gas, that is formed from the remains of prehistoric plants or animals.

garbage patch A mass of plastic garbage floating in the sea drawn together by ocean currents.

ghost gear Nets and other fishing equipment dumped at sea.

greenhouse effect The way that certain gases in the atmosphere stop heat from the Sun from escaping back into Space, warming up the Earth.

greenhouse gases Gases in the Earth's atmosphere, especially carbon dioxide and methane, that play a part in the greenhouse effect.

gyre A rotating circular pattern of ocean currents.

HDPE High-density polyethylene. A strong plastic used to make many things, including kitchenware, crates, and milk containers.

incineration Destruction of garbage by burning it.

landfill A hole or pit dug to be filled with waste.

LDPE Low-density polyethylene. This is a plastic used to make food trays, long-life plastic bags, and squeezable bottles.

leachate Liquid that has passed through a landfill site and usually contains polluting chemicals.

microbeads Tiny solid plastic balls added to some cosmetics, such as face scrubs and body washes.

microfibers A very thin strand or piece of plastic fiber.

microplastic Tiny pieces of plastic measuring ¼ inch or less in length.

molecule A group of atoms bonded together. Everything is made of molecules.

monomer A molecule that can be bonded, or joined, to identical molecules to form a polymer.

naphtha A liquid made from refining oil. Used in many plastics.

nurdle A very small pellet of plastic used as a raw material to make plastic products.

nylon A human-made plastic that is commonly spun into fibers for making fabric, fishing lines, and nets.

oilfield An area under the Earth's surface that contains a large amount of oil.

PET Polyethylene terephthalate, a clear, strong, lightweight plastic used to make recyclable bottles.

pollution When a substance with harmful effects is found in or added to an environment.

polyester A group of different polymer materials often used to make fabrics.

polymer Something made from long chains of molecules. Plastics are polymers.

polystyrene A type of plastic often expanded by blowing air through it to form light molded packaging.

PP Polypropylene, a tough plastic that resists chemicals.

PVC Polyvinyl chloride, one of the most commonly produced plastics. Used for piping, shoes, and clothing.

recycling When used or waste material is turned into something that can be used again.

refinery A place where crude oil is processed and turned into useful products, such as gasoline.

resources Things useful to humans, such as raw materials, air, water, and energy.

sewage system A system of drains and pipes that carry waste and wastewater away for cleaning at a sewage treatment plant.

single-use Something that is used just once then thrown away.

synthetic An object, substance, or material that has been made by humans. Some synthetic products are designed to look like natural ones.

thermoplastics Plastics that soften when heated and harden when they cool down.

UPVC Unplasticized polyvinyl chloride. This plastic is used as a building material, especially for window frames and pipes.

vacuum forming A way of forming an object by sucking a sheet of plastic around a mold.

waterways Rivers, streams, canals, or other narrow routes used for water travel.

Index

A
aluminum 11, 62
atom 20

B
bacteria 8, 44, 53
Bakelite 21
bans 49, 54–55
biodegrading 8–9, 62, 63
blow molding 30

C
campaigns 54, 66, 67
Challenger Deep 38
chemicals 8, 12, 13, 15, 23
    harm to health 13, 23,
      46–47
cleaning up 13, 49, 50–53,
    67, 68
climate change 16, 17
compression molding 31
crude oil 17, 22

D
decomposers 8, 9
distillation tower 22
dumping 33, 35, 36, 38

E
Earth 17, 22
    atmosphere 14, 17
ecosystems 6
energy 16, 17
extraction 16, 22
extrusion 30

F
food chain 40, 41, 46–47
fossil fuels 17, 22, 23, 62

G
garbage patches 42–43
ghost gear 35, 38, 39
greenhouse effect 16
greenhouse gases 14, 15, 17
    methane 14, 15
gyres 42

L
landfill 11, 14–15, 60, 68
leachate 15
litter 10, 12–13, 33, 34–35, 39
living things 12–13, 14, 17,
    44–46
    harm by plastic 6, 12, 13, 15,
      16, 36, 38, 39, 41, 44–45

M
microbeads 37, 62
microfibers 37
microplastics 11, 13, 36–37,
    38, 41, 43, 46–47, 53
molecule 20, 61
monomer 20

N
naphtha 22–23
nurdles 23, 36, 61

O
oil 16, 22, 62
    spills 16
oilfield 17

P
plastic 6, 7, 18, 19, 21, 27, 32,
    40, 56
    advantages of 8, 25–31
    alternatives to 21, 54, 57,
      62–63
    fire risks 12, 15
    in medicine 28, 54
    in the ocean 32–47
    natural 20–21, 62–63
    packaging 11, 28–29, 55,
      59, 69
    problems 6–17
    production 7, 16, 19,
      22–23, 32
    transport of 17, 23, 29,
      34–35
plastic, types of
    ABS 26
    acrylic 26
    ASA 27
    HDPE 51, 60, 61
    LDPE 20, 26, 27, 60
    nylon 26
    PET 11, 20, 50, 60, 61
    polycarbonate 27
    polyester 26
    polypropylene (PP) 26,
      51, 60

    polystyrene 11, 27, 29,
      36, 60
    polyurethane 27
    PVC 26, 30, 60
    thermoplastics 30
    UPVC 27
pollution 10, 12–13, 15,
    38–39, 41
polymer 20, 23

R
recycling 9, 14, 60–61, 67, 69
refinery 22
refining 16, 22
resources 10, 16–17
    nonrenewable 16
reusables 26, 55, 58, 59, 68
rubber 19, 20, 21, 36

S
sewage systems 34
single-use plastic 7, 10–11, 54,
    58, 69
synthetic 19, 21

T
technology 51, 52–53
3D printing 31

V
vacuum forming 30

W
waste 7, 14–15
waterways 11, 33, 34–35, 51

EARTHAWARE
K I D S

Copyright © EarthAware Kids, 2023

Published by EarthAware Kids
A subsidiary of Insight International, L.P.
PO Box 3088
San Rafael, CA 94912
www.insighteditions.com

CEO: Raoul Goff

Created by Weldon Owen Children's Books
Editor: George Maudsley
Designer: Claire Cater
Senior Production Manager: Greg Steffen
Art Director: Stuart Smith
Publisher: Sue Grabham

ISBN: 978-1-64722-611-4

Manufactured, printed and assembled in China
First printing May 2023 TOP0523
27 26 25 24 23 1 2 3 4 5